ROME IN HISTORY

The legend of the foundation of Rome

The birth of Rome is still surrounded by legends. Many different opinions or theories, some of them very imaginative, have been put forward but, at the end, the myth which attributes to Romulus and to Remus the merit of the foundation of Rome, has prevailed. According to this myth, at the fall of Troy, a group of survivors led by Aeneas, son of Anchises, the last king of Troy, landed on the coast of Latium, after a long and perilous journey — narrated by Virgil in the "Aeneid" —. Aeneas was welcome by the king of the Latins who gave him both the throne and his daughter. At the death of his father, Ascanius, son of Aeneas, founded Alba Longa and made it the capital of the little Latin kingdom. Ascanius governed wisely and twelve other kings succeeded him. The last one, however, was a usurper. In fact, Amulius reached the throne after eliminating his brother Numitor and forcing the daughter of the latter to become a Vestal Virgin.

The Vestal Virgins, the guardians of the fire, were bound to remain virgin but Rea Silvia was loved by the god Mars and had two sons of him. She gave them the name of Romulus and Remus. However, Amulius found the two little children, had them put into a basket and abandoned on the current of the Tiber. But they did not die. The basket got entangled in the reeds along the shore, near the Palatine Hill. A wolf took them and fed them.

Later the two children were brought up by two shepherds and having become adult they thought to build a town on the place which had been the witness of their terrible adventure.

However, the plan was a source of dissension between the two brothers and during a quarrel Romulus killed Remus, thus remaining master of the field. He founded a town to which he gave the name of Rome. Legend tells us that it was the 21st April 753 B.C. At once Rome became a town open to exiles and refugees from the neighbouring towns. There was, however, a dearth of women. A remedy to this situation was the famous rapt of the Sabines, to which a war between the Latins and the Sabines followed. The peace that ensued virtually sanctioned the fusion of the Latins with the Sabines. In fact, Rome began to be governed alternatively by a Latin king and by a Sabine king.

The legend of the seven kings

The **first king** was Romulus and he was succeeded by Numa Pompilius, a Sabine. This king dedicated himself to the expansion of the town, which, at the end of the reign of Romulus, already stretched as far as the Viminal and the Esquiline Hills. The **third king** was **Tullus Hostilius**, a Latin who conquered Alba Longa and reduced its inhabitants to slavery, confining them on the Celian Hill. With **Ancus Martius**, the **fourth king** of Rome, the city expanded still further. New dwelling-houses were erected on the Aventine to make place for the increasing population.

Legend tells us that about 616 B.C. Rome had extended on five of the seven famous Hills. With **Ancus Martius** the dynasty of the Latin-Sabine kings came to an end and that of the Etruscan kings began. The first Etruscan king and the **fifth of Rome** was **Tarquinius Priscus** also called the „Old Man". We owe him the construction of the Circus Maximus, the Cloaca Maxima and the first settlement on the Capitoline Hill with the erection of the Temple of Jupiter. **Servius Tullius**, the **sixth king** of Rome, completed the expansion of Rome by occupying the Quirinal. Then, between 578 and 535, he enclosed Rome with walls, which are known as the "Servian Walls". **Tarquinius Superbus**, the **seventh and last king** of Rome, ingloriously ended the Etruscan monarchy and the monarchical period, driven out by the people because of the misdeeds of his son Sextus who, as a last act of violence, had violated the virtuous Lucrezia, wife of Tarquinius Collatinus.

The history of republican Rome

The monarchy, then, was extinguished in 509 B.C. and at the same time the republic was born. And with the republic Rome decisively entered history. The legend of the birth of Rome has in itself some valid historical elements. In fact, it has been proved that Rome originates from a settlement of shepherds and peasants on the Palatine Hill. And Romulus was brought up by a shepherd.

Such a settlement — in forms and in times still partly unknown — was gradually extended to take in the other hills absorbing the primitive villages which had been built on them. For example, on the Palatine, two villages lived together: the "Palatium" and the "Germalus"; the villages of "Oppius", "Cispius", "Gagutal" cohabited on the Esquiline, and so on. An alliance was made between the villages on the Palatine and on the Esquiline — and probably also on the Celian — to defend themselbes against the neighbouring peoples. Such an alliance, which concerned seven villages, was called "Septimontium". The "Roma Quadrata" (the square Rome), the foundation of which is attributed to Romulus on the Palatine, really existed already before the first Millennium B.C., while the villages on the Esquiline belong to the hypothetical Romulean age (VIIIth Century B.C.).

As we can see, there is a continuous overlapping of historical with legendary elements and in order to avoid any perplexity we would like to draw an outline of the situation regarding the famous **"seven kings"**. First of all, we have to point out that the original, political institution was certainly monarchical, but the number of kings was much larger than that which has come down to us from legend.

Among these seven kings, however, Servius Tullius, Tarquinius Superbus and Tullus Hostilius were certainly historical; Numa Pompilius probably historical while Romulus and Ancus Martius were legendary.
History has, therefore, done justice to the merits of some historical kings. According to modern history ,the famous "Servian Walls" were erected at least two centuries after the age of Servius Tullius and hence during a republican epoch: in fact, many historians are calling them the "Republican Walls".

Conquest of the mediterranean countries

Having successfully overcome the difficult phase of the beginning after the revolt led by Tarquinius Collatinus, republican Rome officially entered history. After reducing to submission the Etruscans and the Latins rebellious to the new Roman power; silencing the neighbouring peoples which came down from the nearby mountains; getting over the trying period of the gallic occupation during which Rome was laid waste by **Brennus** (390 B.C.), Rome extended its dominion first over Latium and then over the whole of central Italy. At the same time, domestic strifes for the equality of rights between Plebeians and Patricians were raging in Rome; such strifes, lasting over two centuries, ended only in 287.
After eliminating Pompey in Thessaly and suppressing the last republican resistances of Labenus and Cato, Caesar had himself made, first, "Dictator" and, then, "Pontifex Maximus". In short, all the powers which used to belong to the Senate and the Consuls became concentrated in Caesar's hands.

The birth of the Roman Empire

The plan of Caesar to create an empire, compact, cosmopolitan and universal, founded on justice and equality of rights seemed to take shape. However, great historical events presuppose a period of preparation. Neither the world at large, nor Caesar's collaborators were yet ready to accept his new ideas. The wave of Caesarian reforms abolishing many privileges antagonized many of his collaborators who joined the conspiracy of Brutus and Cassius. And on March 15, 44 B.C., that is, on the Ides of March, Caius Julius Caesar was stabbed to death by the conspirators who thus put and end to the active life of the first "Great Man" in Roman History.

A triumvirate received the heredity of Caesar, but the beneficiary of it was finally Caesar Octavian, the adoptive son of Julius Caesar, who together with Aemilius Lepidus had formed the leading group. The struggle for the succession to Caesar began: a return to the republican institutions being no longer possible and a three-man leadership of the Empire neither. Octavian eliminated his triumvirs one after the other and in 27 he was made "Augustus", that is "Emperor".

Augustus made Rome the true capital of an empire. He reigned really from 27 B.C. to 10 A.D. (that is 41 years) and was succeeded by Tiberius (14-34) then Caligula (34-41) and Claudius I (41-54). With Nero, who entered history especially for the great fire which destroyed the city in 64, the Julius-Claudius dynasty became extinguished. It was the year 68. The death of Nero at only 31 years of age caused the first dynastic crisis. In 69 four emperors were simultaneously elected. After a struggle with his rival Vitellius, Vespasian, elected by the eastern legions, prevailed over all the others.

Vespasian, who belonged to the lineage of the Flavians, was a farsighted and generous emperor. We owe him the construction of the Temple of Jupiter Capitolinus, the Colosseum (which is also called the "Theatre of the Flavians), and the Temple of Peace ect. He was succeeded in 79 by his son Titus who governed only two years. In 81 Titus's brother, Domitian, a capable but evil man, who was made a God, became emperor. A conspiracy got rid of him in 96 and with him the Flavian lineage disappeared. Power passed into the hands of the Antonines, whose first representative, Nerva, began one of the most important periods of imperial Rome.

Nerva, a weak and incapable man, was helped in government administration by Trajan who succeeded him as soon as in 97, and became one of the greatest emperors in Roman History 997-117). Adrian succeeded Trajan (117-138 A.D.) then came Antoninus Pius (138-161) and finally Marcus Aurelius (161-180). Under these four emperors Rome experienced its best period. However, with Marcus Aurelius began also the slow decline which ended three centuries later. The successor of the great Marcus Aurelius was Commodus who accelerated the crisis of the Antonine dynasty. He was killed in a conspiracy and left the throne to Septimius Severus (193-211) who was replaced by his own son, Caracalla (211-217). Then the throne passed to the foolish Heliogabalus who further undermined the stability of the Empire already on the brink of ruin.

The fall of the Roman Empire

During this chaotic period emperors followed each other in rapid succession, there was even three of them simultaneously, until Decius (249-251) was successful in putting a stop to the disintegration of the Empire. Other successful emperors were Valerian (253-260) and his son Gallienus, who kept the Empire together. Diocletian took the Imperial seat to Nicodemia (Turkey). His successor, Constantine the Great, fixed it definitively in Constantinople. Rome fell into decadence and, after knowing the splendours of the IInd century with more than one million inhabitants, became a province town with less than one hundred thousand. Imperial Rome went out of history in 476 A.D.

5

1) VIEW OF THE ROMAN FORUM

Monuments of ancient Rome

We have seen how Rome was born on the Palatine. Its political and social life, however, took place in the **Roman Forum**, that is, within that area which lies at the foot of the Palatine and extends as far as the Velian (on the top of which stands the Temple of Venus and Rome) and the Esquiline, where Nero had the famous "Domus Aurea" (The Golden House) built.

The photograph (1) shows us a beautiful view of the Roman Forum towards the Capitol and the Victorian. It became a site for monuments under Julius Caesar and reached its greatest splendour under Augustus. The Senate, the Popular Consultations, the Tribunals (the famous Basilicae),

the Temples and the Monuments erected to commemorate Consuls and Emperors, all had their seat in the Forum.

When entering the Roman Forum from via dei Fori Imperiali, we have, on the right, the "**Basilica Emilia**" (a) built by Aemilius Lepidus and Fulvius Nobilior in 179 B.C. Immediately after the **basilica**, stands the "**Curia**" (b) erected by the third king of Rome, Tullius Hostilius. It was destroyed several times but always rebuilt (by Sulla in 80; by Caesar in 45 B.C. and by Diocletian in 290 A.D.). In the Middle Ages, it was converted into a church (S. Adriano) and then restored to its original form and level between 1900 and 1937. On the northern side of the "**Piazza del Foro**" (c) stands the "**Column of Phocas**" and the "**Arch of Septimius Severus**" (d and e), the latter half hidden by the three masterly and surviving columns of the "**Temple of Castor and Pollux**" or of the "**Dioscuri**" (f).

6

2) THE ARCH OF SEPTIMIUS SEVERUS AND COLUMN OF THE EMPEROR PHOCAS

In the photo, below on the right, we can also see the columns of the "Temple of Vesta" (g) and adjoining, the remains of the "Temple of Caesar" (h). On the left side, in the photo, there is the area of the "Basilica Giulia" (i) behind which we see the "Portico dei Dei Consenti" (l), the "Temple of Saturn" (m) and the "Temple of Vespasian" (n).

The "Arch of Septimius Severus" (2) is the most important of the existing triumphal arches (m. 25 x 23). It was erected on the Xth anniversary of the ascent to the throne of that Emperor. The "Column of Phocas" (always photo 2), on the other hand, goes back to 608 B.C. and is a present by the first Exarch of Ravenna, Smaragdo, to the eastern Emperor Phocas, who had

3) THE TEMPLE OF SATURN

4) THE TEMPLE OF CASTOR AND POLLUX OR DIOSCURI

The **"Temple of the Vestal Virgins"** is of very ancient origin, for the worship of fire goes back to legendary times. The actual disposition of the monument dates from the time of Septimius Severus who had it rebuilt in 191 A.D. What we are see-

5) THE TEMPLE OF THE VESTALS

given the Pantheon for Christian worship to the pope Boniface IV. The **Temple of Saturn** dates back to 497 B.C. and, therefore, belongs to the first republican period (photo 3). It was built immediately after the expulsion of the Tarquinians.

The eight magnificent columns, which we are seeing, are all that remains of it. The wonderful fluted columns and the fragment of trabeation of the **"Temple of Castor and Pollux"** (or dei Dioscuri) which appear in the photo (4) date back to the time of Augustus (about 6 A.D.). The original Temple, however, goes back to 484 B.C., hence to the first republican period. It was erected by the son of the dictator Aulus Postumius to fulfil a vow, which his father had made to the "Dioscuri" when they interfered in his favour in the battle by the lake Regillus against the Latins and the Tarquinians.

8

6) THE HOUSE OF THE VESTALS

7) STATUES OF THE VESTALS

8) THE TEMPLE OF ANTONINUS AND FAUSTINA

ing in the photo (4) is the area of the patio of the **"House of the Vestal Virgins"**. The Vestal Virgins were the guardians of the sacred fire. Their obligations involved keeping alight the sacred fire in the sacellum and maintaining their vow of chastity. The origin of the Vestal Virgins if of great antiquity. And one has to remember that Romulus, the mythical founder of Rome, was born of a Vestal Virgin. On both sides of the atrium stood magnificent statues of Vestal Virgins (7) and in one of these one seems to recognise the Vestal Claudia who was converted to Christianity.

The service of the Vestal Virgins lasted exactly 30 years and, as we know, if they violated their vow of chastity, they were buried alive.

The **"Temple of Antoninus and Faustina"** (8) was erected b the Emperor Antoninus Pius (138-161 A.D.) to commemorate his wife Faustina, who died very young and was deified by her husband. The "Faustina" in Roman history are two: one called "Faustina Maggiore" who was the wife of Antoninus Pius, and the second named "Faustina Minore" who was the daughter of the first and an Empress, too.

10) THE PALATINE WITH THE CIRCUS MAXIMUS

The **"Arch of Titus"** which stands on the top of the Velian was erected by Domitian (or by Trajan) to commemorate the emperors Vespasian and Titus victorious in the war against the Jews. The **"Sacra Via"** (9) of which one can see a part of the metal, is the road which crosses the whole Forum from the Arch of Titus to the Basilica Giulia. **"The Palatine"** (10) has been the cradle of Rome. In the course of time, it became the residence of the Emperors and of the important persons in Rome. The palaces of Tiberius, those of the Flavian dynasty and the famous "Domus Aurea" were erected beside the houses of Cicero, Crassus and Clodius. In the photo, one can see the **Servian constructions** facing the **"Circus Maximus"**.

The **Forum of Trajan** was one of the largest and most beautiful places in Rome. In the photo (11) we can see the famous „**Mercati Traianei**" (Trajan Markets) which represent a magnificent example of mercantile building in Imperial Rome.

The large atrium in the form of a basilica, whose magnificence one can dimly see, sheltered what in modern terms would be called the "Bargaining Hall".

The shops were within the two hemispheres — one of which is still visible — and the

12) THE TRAJAN COLUMN AND THE CHURCH OF S. MARIA DI LORETO   13) THE RUINS OF THE BASILICA OF MAXENTIUS (or of Constantin)

various floors were connected by numerous stairs. This building block was conceived by Trajan — on a design by the architect Apollodorus of Damascus — for retailing and the distributions of food and gifts to the population.

Of the spacious **Trajan Forum**, besides the already seen markets only the famous **Trajan Column** (12) and the colonnade of the **Basilica Ulpia** remain, the whole against the harmonious background of the church of S. Maria di Loreto.

From what we have seen before (Mercati) and what we are seeing now, we can get a fairly good idea of what was the **"Trajan Forum"** like. Witnesses tell us that it was the most magnificent forum in ancient Rome. One went into it through a Triumphal Arch. At the centre of the square stood a gilded bronze statue of the emperor Marcus Ulpius Trajan (98-117 A.D.).

The **"Basilica of Maxentius"** or of Constantine (13) was one of the most imposing constructions in the Forum and the grandeur of the ruins bears witness of this. Started by the emperor Maxentius after 308, it was finished by Constantine between 312 and 315.

13

14) THE COLOSSEUM

Maxentius was emperor of the Romans from 306 to 312 A.D. but he was so in opposition to a "Tetrarchy" which had taken power at the abdication of his father Maximinus (the tetrarchy was formed by the same Maximinus, by Diocletian, Galerius and Constans). Constantine the Great came to Rome and defeated him at the Milvian bridge.

The **"Colosseum"** or **"Amphitheatrum Flavium"** (14-15) was begun — as we have already seen — by the emperor Vespasian towards 72 A.D. and completed by his son Titus. 188 m. in length, 156 m. in width and 57 m. in height, it was capable of holding more than 87.000 spectators. The greatest games and spectacles took place in it. During the opening games which lasted hundred days, more than 5000 animals and several hundred gladiators are said to have been killed. In 249, the first millenary of the foundation of Rome was celebrated there by mag-

15) THE COLOSSEUM

16) THE COLOSSEUM: INTERIOR OF THE ARENA

17) THE COLOSSEUM: INTERIOR OF UNDERGROUND PASSAGES

nificent games and spectacles. More than 1000 couples of gladiators fought each other and more than 200 animals: elephants, tigers, lions, elks, wild horses and donkeys, hyenas, hippopotamus, girafes, were killed. In 442 the structure was damaged by the earthquake and in the Middle Ages it was plundered as a quarry of travertine blocks. In fact, 100.000 cubic meters of them were used in its construction. Here is what remains of the interior of the Colosseum, in the part that was the arena (16) as well as of the passages for the gladiators and wild animals (17).

The name of Colosseum should have been derived from the huge statue of Nero, which stood in front of the great building structure (see on page 30 in Rome rebuilt the photo 40) and is known as the "Statue of the Colossus". We know that it was erected on the site of the little artifical lake of the "Domus Aurea" of Nero, between the Palatine and the Oppian Hills and that on the first floor of the amphitheatre was the podium of the Emperor as well as that of the Vestal Virgins and the Senators.

The „**Arch of Constantine**" (18), which the Roman Senate and the people dedicated to Constantine after his victory over Maxentius at **Ponte Milvio** (The Milvian Bridge) (315 A.D.), is one of the best-preserved architectural structures in Rome. It is a composite work built with fragments taken from other monuments of Trajan, Adrian, Marcus Aurelius. For example, the eight corinthian columns which form its structure are of the time of Domitian (51-91 A.D.).

The "**Theatre of Marcellus**" (19) is a classic example of republican architecture, which subsequently served as a model for the

18) THE ARCH OF CONSTANTINE

19) THE THEATRE OF MARCELLUS

21) THE TEMPLE OF VESTA

Colosseum which was built nearly a century later. It was begun by Julius Caesar and brought to conclusion in A.D. 13 by Augustus, who dedicated it to his nephew and son-in-law Claudius Marcellus who died very young .

Ten thousand spectators could be accomodated in the theatre which underwent various alterations and was destined to different uses in the course of the centuries. The actual arrangement is due to the Orsini family who has been living in it since 1712. The "**Temple of Apollo Sosianus**" stands quite near the Theatre. Erected in 435 B.C. it was subsequently rebuilt by the Consul Sosius from which it took its name. Proceeding along the Via del Teatro di Marcello, we arrive on the **Piazza Bocca della Verità** where we find the "**Temple of the Vesta**" (21) which owes its name to its circular plan, similar to that of the Temple of the Vestal Virgins in the Forum. Belonging to the Augustan time (perhaps even anterior to), it was converted into a church in the Middle Ages, and was then called S. Stefano delle Carrozze.

22) THE TEMPLE OF FORTUNA VIRILIS

23) THE BATHS OF CARACALLA

24) THE PYRAMIDE OF CAIUS CESTIUS AND THE PORTA OF ST PAUL

Still in Piazza Bocca della Verità stands the **"Temple of Fortuna Virilis"** (22) erected in A.D. 100 and considered a rare example of Greco-Italian architecture. The name is not historical but of popular derivation. In the same square, towards **S. Giorgio in Velabro**, lies also the interesting Arch of Janus which dates from the age of Constantine. From the Piazza Bocca della Verità, proceeding along Via dei Cerchi and across Piazza di Porta Capena, we arrive at the **"Baths of Caracalla"** also called "Baths of Antoninus".

They are a very large and imposing architectural structure. Begun by Septimius Severus in A.D. 206, they were brought to conclusion by his son Caracalla in 217. They were capable of holding 1600 bathers at a time and were definitively damaged by the Gothic invasion.

The **"Pyramid of Caius Cestius"** (24) is one of the most remarquable and best-pre-served monuments of Roman antiquity. Built during the first Imperial period (12 B.C.) it received the mortal remains of Caius Cestius, one of the richest tribunes in Rome. The pyramide rises 121 feet high with a base 100 feet wide. Caius Cestius was an epulone who had charge of solemn banquets.

The **"Pantheon"** (25) is considered one of the most important and significant monuments of ancient Rome. It was erected by Marcus Agrippa in 27 B.C. and was dedicated to the seven "Planetary Gods" (Pantheon means most holy place). Various times damaged and always restored, it was presented to the Pope Boniface 1V by the Emperor of the east in A.D. 609. The Pope dedicated it to the Blessed Virgin and to all Martyrs. The interior is majestic in its matchless grandeur and harmony. The diameter of the rotunda and the height of the Dome are exactly the same: 142 feet. The half-spherical calotte covering the rotunda is the largest ever built (photo 25).

The Pantheon rises in the **Piazza della Rotonda**, in the centre of which lies the Fontana della Porta (1578) surmounted by the **"obelisk of Rameses the Great"** (obelisco egizio) (26) which was found, like the „**Pulcin of Minerva**" (27), among the ruins of the "Iseo Campense". From the Pantheon to the **Piazza della Minerva** is only a short way and here, facing the **Church of S. Maria Sopra Minerva**, is the second **"Obelisco Egizio"** for which Ferrata (1667) carved — on a design by Bernini — the marmoreal base of the little elephant familiarly called **"Il Pulcino della Minerva"** by the people.

The **"Tomb of Cecilia Metella"** (28) lies at the IIIrd km of the Ancient Appian Way **(Via Appia Antica)** and is among the best-known monuments in Rome, probably because of the suggestiveness of the place where it rises. It was built by Quintus Metellus for his beloved daughter Cecilia.

ROME RECONSTRUCTED

One of the most interesting featurees of archeology is that it can, within certain limits, offer us often very precise pictures of a past that is gone. Of course, what has been completely obliterated can be reconstructed only by the imagination, whereas, when certain vestiges and remains can be seen, a very exact reconstruction becomes possible — at least in model —. Such a reconstruction has been brought to conclusion by the architect Italo Gismondi of Rome. The work which has lasted 30 years has enabled him to re-make "Rome as it was" in the time of Constantine the Great. This very hard work was begun in 1937 for the "Augustan exhibition of Romanity" (mostra Augustana della Romanità) under the pressure of the times which wanted to

27) THE "PULCIN OF MINERVA"

26) THE PANTHEON: THE EXTERNAL FRONT AND THE OBELISK

translate everything into terms of imperial power and which drew from the Roman past a mania for grandeur which the present did not give and did not justify.

Of that "mania for grandeur", the plastic model of Gismondi is the only serious and useful thing for a better understanding of Rome. It is really the unique, true and authentic "Rome as it was" which can be looked at with respect and can, therefore, appear in publications which, like ours, are made for the intelligent tourist who wants to form for himself a most complete idea of Rome. Naturally, we have not abandoned the purely imaginative reconstructions of Rome, but we have entrusted them to the skill of a painter who has clothed them in a particularly efficacious expressiveness. Here beneath, we show you a reconstruction of the "Roman Forum" (29) seen by a painter. In the two following pages we offer you a splendid view of the whole Imperial Rome, of that city which in the second century A.D. had already one million inhabitants and was, therefore, the largest town in the world.

21

28) THE TOMB OF CECILIA METELLA ON THE ANCIENT APPIAN WAY ▶

29) THE ROMAN FORUM

Here, below, is the **"Roman Forum"** as it was, and above, as it is now. (1) the Arc of Septimius Severus, (2) the Curia, (3) the Basilica Emiliana, (4) the Temple of Antoninus and Faustina, (5) the Basilica of Maxentius, (6) the Colosseum, (7) the Temple of Venus and Rome, (8) the Column of Phocas, (9) the Temple of the Vestals, (10) the House of the Vestals, (11) the Temple of Caesar, (12) the Temple of Castor and Pollux, (13) the Basilica Giulia, (14) the Arch of Titus, (15) the Temple of Saturn.

29 bis) RECONSTRUCTION OF THE ROMAN FORUM

30) FIGHT OF GLADIATORS IN THE ARENA OF THE COLOSSEUM

33) THE COLOSSEUM (in Gismondi's reconstruction) ▶

31) MARTYRDOM OF CHRISTIANS IN THE COLOSSEUM

Looking at the plastic model from the illustrations that follow one becomes aware of the complexitiy, difficulty and greatness of the work accomplished in three decades by Italo Gismondi and his team. Nothing has been left to chance and the technician has behaved before ancient Rome as one would behave before a town "to be built on scale", that is to say, everything in its exact proportions for a technico-historical parameter among the most difficult ones to make. The plastic model, which we are publishing, deserves the whole attention of our readers, because it is not easy to find it in other publications of the kind.

The following are two scenes of life in the Colosseum during the Imperial period. The **"Fight of Gladiators"** (30) and the **"Extermination of Christians"** (31) representing two dramatic phases of as many historical vicissitudes. On the page in front of you, your can see the careful architectural reconstruction of the **"Colosseum and of the Arch of Constantine"** (33) due to Italo Gismondi.

26

34) THE BASILICA OF MAXENTIUS OR OF CONSTANTINE (Gismondi)

35) THE BASILICA OF MAXENTIUS DURING AN AUDIENCE

36) THE HOUSE OF THE VESTALS

On these two pages, there is at number (34) the **"Basilica of Maxentius"** (or of Constantine) reconstructed by Gismondi: observe the classic construction, divided into a nave and two aisles by massive piers, whose features can still be dimly seen (page 13). On the plates (35) and (36), the painter shows us the interior of the **"Basilica of Maxentius"** and of the **"House of the Vestals"** with scenes of the life of the epoch. On this page, there is a beautiful detail of the **"Forum of Augustus"** (37) with the Temple of Mars Ultor (that is, Mars the avenger) erected to commemorate the victory of Augustus at Philippi over Brutus and Cassius, the killers of Caesar. The other detail shows us the **"Forum of Trajan"** (38), still in the reconstruction of Gismondi. Notice the famous **"Column"**, the **"Basilica Ulpia"** and the spacious amphitheatre with the colonnade of the **"Mercati Traianei"**.

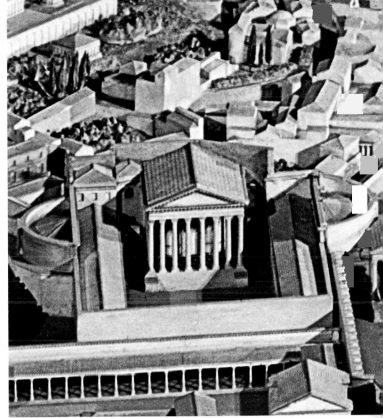

37) THE FORUM CF AUGUSTUS (in Gismondi's reconstruction)

38) THE FCRUM OF TRAJAN WITH THE COLUMN (In Gismondi's reconstruction)

On the site of the fabulous **Domus Aurea** of Nero, Trajan erected his **"Baths"** (39) of which some traces still remain on the Oppian Hill. More important vestiges of the Domus Aurea are, on the other hand, still in existence.

The **"Temple of Venus and Rome"** (40) was one of the largest edifices for worship in Rome. Today only the two apsides facing the Colosseum remain. In the reconstruction of Gismondi we can also see the statue of the Colossus.

The **"Circus Maximus"** was

39) THE BATHS OF TRAJAN (In Gismondi's reconstruction)

40) THE TEMPLE OF VENUS AND ROME WITH THE STATUE OF THE COLOSSUS (In Gismondi's reconstruction)

41) THE CHARIOT-RACE IN THE CIRCUS MAXIMUS

42) VIEW OF THE ROMAN FORUM (in Gismondi's reconstruction)

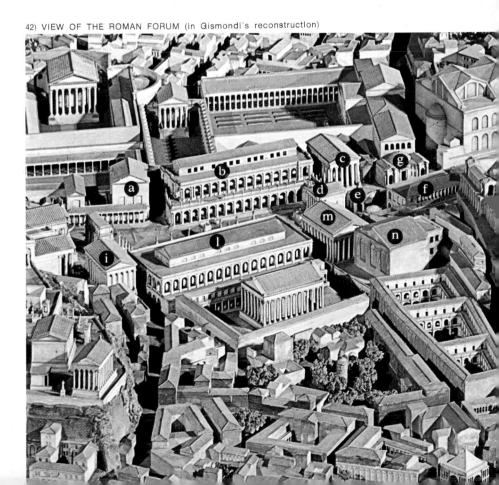

the centre of very important demonstrations and spectacles. Among the most famous was the **"Chariot-Race"** (41) reconstructed here by a painter. Here, on the side, is a faithful reconstruction by Gismondi of a part of the **"Roman Forum"** (42): one can notice in order from the left: the Curia (a), the Basilica Emilia (b), the Temple of Antoninus and Faustina (c), the Temple of Caesar (d), the Temple of the Vestals (e), the House of the Vestals (f), the Temple of the Divine Romulus (g), the Forum of Peace (h), the Temple of Saturn (i), the Basilica Giulia (l), the Temple of Castor and Pollux (m), and the Temple of Augustus (n).

ROME IN CHRISTIANITY

During a certain period of its history, the civilization of Rome moved forward in a parallel direction with the civilization which was imposing the Church of Christ. The two civilizations did not have an easy coexistence but in the long run they influenced and complemented each other in such a way as to offer to the world once again — after the imperial splendours — the image of Rome as the moral capital of the world.

The first Christian community of Rome was formed about A.D. 50 and the Apostle Peter was its head. He suffered a martyr's death in 64 or 67 of the Christian era, but the Church had already laid the foundations of its success. It was not, however, an easy success. In the unavoidable collision between the rights of the Church and the will of the pagan state, it was the Church which had to bear the first hard consequences: from Nero to Domitian; from Trajan to Adrian and Antoninus Pius and Marcus Aurelius and Septimius Severus down to Diocletian, Maximinus and Galerius, the first Christian communities have experienced hard persecutions. In fact, we must reach the time of Constantine the Great to find peace between Pagan and Christian Rome (Constantine Peace of Milan in 313).

Though he had his residence in the faraway Constantinople, the Emperor's support speeded up the process of conversion of the Italian peoples and in 382 the Emperor Gratian gave up the title of "Pontifex Maximus". Finally, in 394, all Pagan rites and ceremonies were forbidden and the "fundamental truths" of the faith were laid down against the nascent heresies and in particular against that of Arius who denied the divinity of Christ.

The Church asserted its supremacy as a bulwark of civilisation and as a cohesive force never more so than during the barbaric invasions. After the fall of the Roman Empire, Italy and Europe were able to recover owing to the support of the Church. A period of order and peace followed the post-imperial chaos and this enabled Gregory the

Great to send emissaries to England and to Germany for a first attempt of evangelization.

By that time, the Church was sovereign in Rome and the Pontiff was not only the head of the Church, but also of the city. The short-lived reestablishment of the Roman Empire of the west, with what may be defined as the "Liturgy" of the crownings of kings and emperors which was reintroduced in Rome by Charlemagne, brought about a moral as well as an economic revival. Unfortunately the Saracens arrived from the Tyrrhenian sea and devastated Rome. Even the Basilicae of St Peter and St Paul were seriously harassed.

The Church, however, persevered in its work and about the XIth century it brought almost to conclusion the evangelization of Europe. In 1084 Rome underwent another invasion from the north. This time it was the Normans who laid waste the city and the destructions of Robert de Guiscard left their mark on the centuries. In Rome everything was bound to the Church and the municipal administration had so little weight or power that when the Pope left Rome for the Avignon residence (1305-1377) the city suffered a hard counter-stroke. Building stopped, goats were grazing on the Capitol and the Roman Forum became the "camp of the cows". It is said that St Peter's Square and the site of St John Lateran became pastures, too. The population of the city dwindled to a mere thirty thousands. After the Avignon phase, the Papal Rome experienced a new, brilliant revival. It was the period of the Renaissance. The Popes, raised to princely dignity in the same manner as the other sovereigns in Italy and elewhere, made Rome the Capital of the Catholic world. Famous artists were called to Rome where there was an impressive eagerness for new works of art. The new Vatican Palaces were erected, the new St Peter's Basilica was built, new roads were opened, new palaces went up, altering completely the appearance of the city. Julius II and Sixtus

V are the popes who, in this period, left a deeper trace in the history and in the soul of the city. We owe them the famous "Via Giulia" and "Via Sistina", but we owe also to Pope Sixtus V the "Via Merulana", that splendid straight route which connects the Basilica of Santa Maria Maggiore with that of St John Lateran.

In the 17th century Rome was embellished with the wonderful Piazza Navona. The "Scalinata della Trinità dei Monti" and the famous "Fountain of Trevi" were built during the 18th century. Rome of the temporal power of the popes over the city, Rome of the 18th century, is more or less, the Rome of today. From the tragic days of the "Sack of Rome" in 1527 when the city was reduced to a shadow of its former self, with a fall of population from 90.000 to 30.000, the Eternal City has constantly progressed, with the support of the Church, till it had 200.000 inhabitants in 1850, which had become 400.000 at the end of the 19th century.

The events of those years were dominated by the dissension between the Italian State and the Catholic Church. The times had changed and with them the political and social conditions of Italy. A conflict between the Church, which did not want to give up its prerogatives and the State which — under the pressure of progress and of political necessity — had become united and could no longer accept a division of power over Italy, became unavoidable. The conflict between State and Church ended in 1929 with the "Conciliation", with which the State guarantied certain liberties to the Church against the renunciation of temporal power by the Church. The Vatican State was born. It consists of the City of Vatican and of the three famous Basilicae: S. Maria Maggiore, St John Lateran and St Paul-outside-the-Walls.

In the following pages, we will show you the Rome of the Basilicae and the churches, with particular attention to St Peter and the Vatican City, which is not only the Holy See from which Peter, keeping high the cross of Christ, sent his call to the world, about two thousand years ago, but also the moral seat of all those men who have seen and see in the Church the bearer of peace on earth among the peoples of good will.

We shall not, of course, neglect a description, even if only a summary one, of the three other patriarchal Basilicae of Rome, in order to accompany our visitors not only on their visits to the most important centres of Christianity but also and above all, since this is the primary function of this book, in their contacts with the architectural, pictorial, ornamental and mosaic marvels of each Basilica. It may be of some interest to know that the "Four Basilicae" of Rome have been erected in different periods, occupying each time a new site of the city. The first basilica is St John Lateran which dates back to A.D. 311-314; the second one is St Peter which was dedicated in 326; the third is the Basilica of St Paul-outside-the-Walls which goes back to 386 whereas the fourth and the last is S. Maria Maggiore, begun in 432 and consecrated in 440. No one of the four Basilicae has kept its original aspect. The old St Peter was completely destroyed at the erection of the new one; St John Lateran changed his façade in 1735, but it had already undergone important modifications especially in 1308 when it was completely rebuilt after a fire; S. Maria Maggiore, too, has been variously modified and the two façades go back respectively to 1676 and 1758; the basilica of St-Paul-outside-the-Walls had gone undamaged through the centuries until 1823 when it was destroyed by a furious fire.

43) SUGGESTIVE SUNSET ON THE TIBER WITH ST PETER IN THE BACKGROUND

44) CASTEL SANT'ANGELO WITH THE SANT'ANGELO BRIDGE

45) ONE OF THE COURTYARDS OF CASTEL SANT'ANGELO

CASTEL SANT'ANGELO

Let us start this visit to the City of Vatican and its Basilicae with a splendid view of St Peter on the Tiber (43). Here, above, there is the "Castel Sant'Angelo" (44). Castel Sant'Angelo or "Mausoleum of Adrian" was built between 135 and 139 by the Emperors Adrian and Antoninus Pius: Adrian had conceived it as his mausoleum and that of his dynasty. In the course of the centuries, it underwent many alterations, among which the addition of four bastions on the tops of the Roman base; the raising of the cylindrical main tower by Benedict IX (1033-44), on which Julius II had the Papal apartments built and the "Bronze Angel" (46) which dominates the city.

ST PETER'S BASILICA

The history of the city of Rome is intimately bound to that of the Holy See: The basilica of St Peter is the most immediate and most fascinating expression of this union. Constantine the Great commanded the construction of the first basilica and he had it erected on the site where St Peter had been buried after suffering a martyr's death. It was begun in 324 and brought to conclusion two years later.

After remaining open for worship more than a thousand years, it was reduced to a ruin and the Pope Nicholas V decided to rebuild it. Julius II assigned the execution of the work to Bramante who began construction in 1506; Raphael continued the work until 1520. Then Michelangelo carried it on from 1546 onwards. The new Basilica was finally consecrated on the 18th November 1626, on the 1300th anniversary of the consecration of the original basilica. The studies of Michelangelo, who died before finishing the work, were continued by other architects and in particular by Giacomo della Porta and Domenico Fontana for the execution of the **cupola.** The new **façade**, erected by Carlo Maderno, was begun in 1607 and

46) THE ANGEL OF CASTEL SANT'ANGELO   47) A VIEW OF THE VIA DELLA CONCILIAZIONE SEEN FROM THE CUPOLA OF ST PETER

48) THE BASILICA OF ST PETER WITH THE MAGNIFICENT SQUARE OF PIAZZA BERNINI

completed in 1614. The works for the lay-out of the **Piazza S. Pietro**, designed by Bernini, began in 1650, and the magnificent square partly enclosed by two semicircular colonnades, consisting of 284 columns and 88 pillars, surmounted by 140 statues of saints, was opened in 1667. In the centre towers an obelisk 82 1/2 feet high, and two fountains complete the harmony of this unique square.

From the point of view of the faith, Rome is the capital of the world. Hundreds of millions of men, and not only catholic, look to it to hear the message of peace and brotherhood which the successors of St Peter periodically send to the world. By losing power on the temporal level, the Church has seen, in the last five decades, its prestige and its moral force as an almost unique organization capable of bringing forward a

discourse clearly free from vested interests, increase enormously. Such a discourse, at first very feeble, has been amplified under the short, but exceptional pontificate of Pope John XXIII (Angelo Roncalli) who has entered into relations with all nations in the world, including those countries which had, in the past, historico-political reasons for feeling aversion towards the Catholic Church.

This discourse received an official form with the results of the Sacred Council which "Papa Giovanni" convened in the last months of his life and which his successor, Pope Paul VI, brought to conclusion thre years later. St Peter's Square and the Vatican are a compulsory goal for all those people who come to Rome in search of the comfort of the Faith or for an intimate contact with the spirituality.

49) A RARE PHOTOGRAPH OF ST PETER AND ITS SQUARE

50) EXIT OF THE COUNCIL FATHERS AFTER A SITTING OF THE SECOND VATICAN COUNCIL

51) PAUL VI SPEAKING TO THE CROWD FROM THE WINDOW OF HIS APARTMENT   52) A BEAUTIFUL VIEW OF ST PETER'S SQUARE

Each year, millions of believers and tourists come together in Rome in order to visit the City and to see from nearby the Vicar of Christ on earth. The pontifical audiences are always thronged and each Sunday, many thousands of believers gather in the square to hear the Pope who appears at the window of his apartment (se photo 51) to bless the multitude.

The most important ecclesiastical event of the last decade has been the **"Second Vatican Ecumenical Council"**, called together by the great Pope John XXIII and brought to conclusion by his successor Pope Paul

VI. The **"Concilio Ecumenico Vaticano Se-condo"** (53) has taken place in the Basilica and, as you can see, the prelates were aligned along both sides of the nave. The "Vatican Second" lasted from 1962 to 1965 and followed at a distance of nearly 100 years the "Vatican First" (1869-1870) which had been convened to establish the dogma of Pontifical infallibility. Paul VI (54) has attended various meetings and has, in any case, followed very attentively the council work.

Paul VI celebrates the Holy Mass in St Peter on the greatest festivities. Of particular splendour are those celebrated during the course of the Holy Week and at Easter.

55) A RATHER RARE PHOTO: PAUL VI CELEBRATING THE MASS ▶

53) A SITTING OF THE COUNCIL

54) PAUL VI ATTENDING A SITTING OF THE COUNCIL

56 bis) JOHN XXIII "THE GOOD POPE"

57) THE CUPOLA SEEN FROM INSIDE

A visit, even a short one, in the interior of the Basilica of St Peter is the most suggestive thing one can imagine. The serene atmosphere of the temple, the singing of the believers, the lights and sometimes the sounds cause unique sensations. Such sensations are also experienced by the tourist who finds himself suddenly lowered into a magic world of sublime beauty (56). The magnificent **"Cupola"** (57) seen from the interior is something exceptional. The Papal Altar is situated under the cupola and leaning against the last pier on the right is the famous and venerated "Bronze Statue of St Peter" (58) popularly called "The black Pope".

44

IOANNES P.P. XXIII

53) THE TOMB OF JOHN XXIII

58) THE BRONZE STATUE OF ST PETER COMMONLY CALLED "THE BLACK POPE"

60) THE MONUMENT TO BENEDICT XIV

THE PIETÀ OF MICHELANGELO

The interior of St Peter is a series of unending stupefying marvels, but probably the most beautiful, certainly the most famous one, is the marble group called the "Pietà" of Michelangelo (61). The young Michelangelo was not vet 25 years old when between 1499 and 1500 he sculptured the "Pietà" on a commission by the Cardinal Jean de Bilhères. The Pietà is situated in the homonymous chapel, immediately after the entrance of **Porta Santa.** In 1972 it had been disfigured by a Hungarian maniac and then restored to its original splendour. In the passage towards the Right Transept stands the **"Monument to Benedict XIV"** (60) and in the **Vatican Grottoes** is the **"Tomb of John XXIII"** (59) together with those of many other Popes.

61) THE PIETÀ

THE VATICAN CITY

THE VATICAN CITY

The "State of the Vatican City" was officially born on the IIth February 1929 after the signature of the famous "Lateran Treaty" which put an end to the secular tension between the State and the Church. This little State has an area of only 108 acres (one-sixth of a square miles) and a population of about one thousand. It consists of the Basilica of St Peter, of the Vatican Palaces with their marvellous gardens. The whole is surrounded by a high wall which can be seen in Via Porta Angelica, Piazza del Risorgimento and Viale Vaticano. The basilica of S. Maria Maggiore, the basilica of St John Lateran and the basilica of St Paul-outside-the-Walls also belong to the state of Vatican and therefore enjoy extra-territoriality. The state of Vatican coins its own money, has its own philatelic emissions and its own broadcasting station. Once it had some armed corps such as the **"Pontifical Gendarmes"** (62), established by Pius VII in 1816, and the **"Swiss Guards"** (64), a corps founded in 1506 which had the duty to keep public order like any other police force. There was also the **"Noble Guards"** (63) and the **"Palatine Guards of Honour"** which performed ceremonial duties.

John XXIII dissolved the corps of honour because no longer suitable to the new conciliatory spirit of the Church, more and more open towards its most humble sons. And Paul VI dissolved the Pontifical Gendarmes keeping alive only the Swiss Guards who are still wearing the splendid 18th century uniforms said to have been designed by Michelangelo.

62) THE POLICE FORCE (POLICE STATION)

63) THE NOBLE GUARDS

64) THE SWISS GUARDS

The Pope is not only the head of the universal Church, but also the head of the state of Vatican with full legislative, executive and judiciary powers which he exercises through the respective organs. As head of the Church he enjoys the "primatus jurisdictionis", that is, he has full power over the Church. The "Sacro Collegio" of the Cardinals and the "Curia Romana" help him in his work. The manifestations of the Vatican City are the **Conclave** with which the new Popes ore elected and the Holy Year **"Anno Santo"** which was held for the first time in 1300 under Boniface VII. According to the rule, it is held every 25 years (the last

dates from 1950) and begins with the opening of the **Porta Sacra** to be found in all the **four Basilicae.** At the end of the Holy Year the doors are walled again.

THE VATICAN GARDENS

Apart from the administration and government buildings you can admire in the interior of the Vatican City, the "Vatican Gardens" deserve particular attention both for the suggestiveness of the surroundings and for the natural and architectural beauties

65) THE GARDENS OF THE VATICAN: THE LOURDES GROTTO

66) THE FOUNTAIN OF THE AQUILONE

67) THE ENGLISH GARDEN

68) THE TOWER OF POPE JOHN

69) THE PONTIFICAL ACADEMY OF SCIENCES OR CASINA OF PIUS IV

you meet with. Entering by the **"Arco delle Campane"** you arrive in **Piazza S. Marta** in close proximity to which is the imitation of the "Grotta di Lourdes" (65). You then take Via delle Fondamenta and arrive at the **Stradone dei Giardini.** In these **gardens** you will find several monuments.

Among these, the **"Fontana dell'Aquilone"** (66), by the Dutch Giovanni Vasanzio who also designed the **Fontana del Sacramento,** deserves particular attention. Also marvellous and lovely are: the **"English Garden"** (67) with its numerous flower-beds and little fountains, the **"Tower of Pope John"** (68) and, above all, the **"Casina of Pius IV"** or **"Pontifical Academy of Sciences"** (69) which is situated exactly in the middle of the gardens. In spite of its name, the very beautiful edifice was begun by Paul IV in

1558 and completed in 1561. In the gardens you should also see the **"Fontana della Galera"** (towards Piazza Risorgimento) and the **Monument to St Peter** which stands in the central part of the gardens, too. In the following page is a splendid view of the **"Dome of St Peter seen from the Gardens"** (70).

This special "view of the Cupola" has a special meaning too. That is, it re-echoes an idea, which could not be realized, of a basilica of St Peter practically rising from the earth: an enormous and splendid Cupola towering in the centre of a square without anything before it to limit its architectural boldness and its sense of elevation towards the sky. But unfortunately, the 17th century façade has destroyed every effect.

51

70) THE CUPOLA SEEN FROM THE VATICAN GARDENS ▶

THE SISTINE CHAPEL

A visit to the "Sistine Chapel", which is one of the most beautiful and well-known halls in the world, is a fundamental step towards an understanding of the Vatican wonders. According to the best qualified critique, the paintings which adorn the chapel constitute "the unsurpassed and insuperable masterpiece of painting of all times" owing to the work of Michelangelo.

The "Chapel" ist a rectangle about 133 feet long, 43 feet wide and 65 1/2 feet high. It was erected by the Pope Sixtus IV — hence the name of Sistine — who entrusted its execution to Giovanni dei Dolci in 1473 and it was completed in 1484. Between 1481 and 1483 Sixtus IV called many great artists to paint the walls of the Chapel and among these we have to mention Pinturicchio, Botticelli, Ghirlandaio, Cosimo Rosselli, Luca Signorelli, Bartolomeo della Gatta, Perugino. The wall in front of the altar has been painted by Fiammingo and Matteo of Lecce over earlier frescoes by Ghirlandaio and Salviati. As we have already noticed, the insuperable masterpieces of the "Sistine Chapel" is the **"Last Judgment"** (71) which we will see in some important details, and the **"Volta"**, both painted by Michelangelo. The "Volta" (the barrel-vaulted ceiling) was commissioned of Michelangelo by Julius II in 1508 and was completed in 1512. It covers an area of about 8281 square feet. For this titanic work: a marvellous amalgam of small and large figures blending into a harmonious and majestic whole, Michelangelo used a new, revolutionary technique of perspective. The **"Last Judgment"**, on the contrary, was painted between 1536 and 1541. This work, Julius II having died, was commissioned of the great artist by Pope Clement VII in 1534. But he, too, died before the begin of the work. However Paul II kept the agreement of his predecessor. As the photo on page 54 shows, in the last judgment "Christ as Judge" appears at the centre of the fresco and near him are the Madonna, St John the Baptist, St Andrew and other Saints. Beneath, on the left, is the group of angels with the trumpets of the judgment, and, sideways, a damned caught by a devil. Still lower, is Charon with his boat full of damned souls going to hell.

As you probably know, the Sistine — which can be easily visited during the indicated time and days — is also the hall where the "Conclavi" for the election of new popes are held and the seat of other important and solemn ceremonies. Over the Sistine is a chimney from which the famous "black smoke" or "white smoke" comes out after each vote for the election of a pope. The smoke is caused by the combustion of the ballot-papers used for the vote; to cause black smoke (no election), wet straw is mixed with the ballot-papers.

To get a better image of the Sistine you have to remember that it stood on the foundations of a sanctuary which Pope Nicholas III erected about 1280. When Michelangelo undertook the work of the decoration of the "Volta", in 1508, he erased an earlier decoration by Piermatteo d'Amelia, which represented a starry heaven. Finally among the remarquable things of the Sistine is the choir, which sings only during the religious functions officiated by the Pope. It consists of 32 singers.

73) THE LAST JUDGMENT: ST JOHN BAPTIST

74) THE LAST JUDGMENT: A DAMNED

75) THE LAST JUDGMENT: THE VISAGE OF THE MADONNA

THE LAST JUDGMENT

In the general view on page 54, you should observe attentively the "Column of the Elect" which is on the right of Christ; beneath, several devils are in vain trying to keep them back, while they are preparing themselves for the ascent to heaven.

In the details we see on this page and on the preceding one of **"Christ as Judge"** (72), we can notice the majesty and the beauty of the fresco. The visages and the attitudes are exceptionally expressive and everything, including the single scenes, is pervaded by the sense of drama of this apocalyptic event. Look carefully at Christ, serene and stern at the same time; at **St John the Baptist** (73) wearing on his face an expression of confident expectation; at

71) THE LAST JUDGMENT: GENERAL VIEW

72) THE LAST JUDGMENT: CHRIST AS JUDGE

76) THE LAST JUDGMENT: THE TRUMPETS OF THE JUDGMENT

77) THE LAST JUDGMENT: CHARON

the Madonna (75) in an attitude of calm participation in the decisions of her divine son; and at "The Damned" on whose face is all the drama of a lost humanity.

Some of the groups composing the Last Judgment are of a rare effective expressivenes. This is especially true of the angels who are blowing the **trumpets of the Last Judgment** (76) to awake the dead and take them before Christ the Judge. The resurrection of the dead is beneath, on the left, whereas Minos is waiting below, on the right, exactly where the souls of the damned are falling. At the centre, beneath, is Charon (77) with his boat, ready to take the damned to hell. Notice also the significant contrast of colours between the airiness of the group of angels and the gloomy colour of Charon.

With regard to the figure of **Minos**, who is at the bottom right hand corner of the fresco, with his tail around his body as in Dante's description, some critics have thought to recognise in him the Master of Ceremonies of Paul III, who objected to the nudity of the figures.

57

78) THE VOLTA: CREATION OF ADAM ▶

79) THE VOLTA: DETAIL OF THE CREATION OF ADAM: THE HANDS

80) THE VOLTA: DETAIL OF THE CREATION OF ADAM: THE VISAGE

THE VOLTA THE CEILING

The famous "Volta of the Sistine", that is the central part of the ceiling, is divided into nine rectangles, each of them illustrating a scene from Genesis or from the Old Testament. We have chosen only a few of these episodes which we think to be the most meaningful ones. The illustrations (78), (79), (80) will show, first the whole painting, and then two beautiful details of the **"Creation of Adam"** (78). Notice the dignity of Adam, the truly fatherly attitude of God surrounded by his angels. In the detail of the "Hands" (79) observe both the precision and the delicacy of the stroke; on the face of Adam (80) there is almost the consciousness of the solemn moment. The **"Flood"** is probably one of the most dramatically expressive paintings of the ceiling: the fragility of the human condition before the breaking loose of the forces of nature and hence before divine decisions is expressed in a masterly manner.

Another of the nine rectangles represents **"God separating light from darkness"** (82). It is the first over the altar, since Genesis

82) THE VOLTA: GOD SEPARATING LIGHT FROM DARKNESS

begins with this episode. The photo (83) will show us one of the twelve lunettes which Michelangelo painted on the curved perimetrical part of the central ceiling: here is the lunette of Zorobabele, an ancestor of Christ. Besides the lunettes along the curved perimeter between the walls and the Volta are twelve "Chairs" every one dedicated to a "Sybil" or to a "Prophet»». On the adjoining page is the **"Chair of the Prophet Isaiah"** (84).

In order to complete this rapid review of the works of Michelangelo in the Sistine Chapel we will show you another lunette: **"Solomon"** (86) which is placed beside the "Chair of Isaiah"; and one of the twelve lunettes above the windows, representing two ancestors of Christ: Roboamus, King of Judea and son of Solomon, and Abias, the second king of Judea. The lunette of Solomon shows the king as a child.

83) THE LUNETTE OF ZOROBABEL

ROBOAM

ABIAS

85) "LUNETTE" OF THE ANCESTORS

86) "LUNETTE" OF SOLOMON

THE VATICAN MUSEUMS

The Vatican Museums, which are housed in the Vatican Palaces, constitute a whole of enormous artistic importance. The importance of these collections is also due to the fact that many Vatican Palaces were erected to house them. The Vatican Museums are composed of the "Pinacoteca" (Vatican Picture Gallery), the "Egyptian Museum" the "Etruscan Museum", the "Museo Pio-Clementino" the "Gallery of the Candelabra" the "Museum of Christian Art", the "Museo Profano" (Museum of pagan antiquities), the "Museum Chiaramonti", the "Sistine Chapel", the "Borgia Rooms", the "Stanze of Raphael", the "Loggia of Raphael" and of other rooms and Galleries. The aim of this book is essential and hence

87) PINACOTECA (PICTURE GALLERY): TRITTICO STEFANESCHI (Giotto)

88) CHAPEL OF NICHOLAS V: SCENES OF THE LIFE OF S. LORENZO (Beato Angelico)

89) CHAPEL OF NICHOLAS: SCENES OF THE LIFE OF S. LORENZO (Beato Angelico)

we shall only give a very short summary of the Vatican Museums.

One of the most beautiful pieces of the "Pinacoteca" is the **"Trittico Stefaneschi"** (87) by Giotto and his pupils and commissioned by the Cardinal Stefaneschi.

After passing the Museum Pio-Clementino, you arrive at the Museum Chiaramonti. Here, in the **new wing**, is the statue of **"Augusto di Prima Porta"** (90), a famous monument found in 1863 at Prima Porta on the Via Flaminia, which represents the Emperor in an oratory attitude. Still in the same room is the statue of the **"Nilo"** (91), a very beautiful hellenistic work found, like the obelisk of the Piazza del Pantheon, at the Iseo Campense in 1513. On the upper floor of the Palace of the Vatican Museums, you should look at the **"Fatti della Vita di S. Lorenzo"** (Scenes of the life of St Laurence) by Beato Angelico (88): S. Lorenzo giving the treasures of the Church to the poors; S. Lorenzo before the Emperor Decius; S. Lorenzo prisoner and S. Lorenzo being stoned.

90) MUSEUM CHIARAMONTI, NEW WING: STATUE OF AUGUSTUS

91) MUSEUM CHIARAMONTI, NEW WING: STATUE OF THE "NILE"

THE BASILICA OF S. MARIA MAGGIORE

After speaking of the most important of the "Four Patriarchal Basilicae" in Rome, here we are at **S. Maria Maggiore** which is situated in the immediate neighbourhood of Termini Station (you need only to proceed along **Via Cavour**). In chronological order, it is the fourth of the Roman Basilicae, since it was erected in 452 by Pope Sixtus III on the Cispian Hill, which is one of the tops of the Esquiline. The date of its construction coincides with the council of Efeso (431) which sanctioned the title of "Mother of God" for the Madonna, hence the basilica is dedicated to S. Maria. In 1288 Pope Nicholas IV rebuilt its **apse**, which is the actual one; in the calotte is a precious mosaic by Torriti, dating from 1295. In 1670 Pope Clement X had the **posterior façade** rebuilt (94). It can be see from Piazza dell'Esquilino and Via Cavour. The romanesque

92) BASILICA OF S. MARIA MAGGIORE: THE EXTERIOR, FROM THE HOMONYMOUS SQUARE

93) BASILICA OF S. MARIA MAGGIORE: THE CENTRAL NAVE

94) BASILICA OF S. MARIA MAGGIORE:
THE EXTERIOR, FROM THE SQUARE OF THE ESQUILINE

bell-tower commanding the splendid construction is the highest (246 feet) in Rome
(92). The very beautiful **nave** (94) shows,
on the wall above the colonnade, splendid
mosaics dating back to the time of Sixtus
III (low Empire). Note also the **caisson
ceiling** and the beautiful pavement by the
Maestri Cosmati, many of whom worked in
Rome during that period.

Near the Basilica is the **Church of San Prassede** — in Via San Martino ai Monti, the
second street on the right of Via Merulana
— which goes back to 822 and which was
commissioned by Pope Paschal I in honour
of Santa Prassede, sister of **S. Pudenziana**
to whom is also dedicated a Church situated in Via Urbana (Piazza dell'Esquilino).
The **"interior"** (96) of the church of Santa
Prassede that can be admired today is
very different from the original one, which
did not have the three transversal arches
over the median aisle.

96) CHURCH OF S. PRASSEDE: INTERIOR

98) CHURCH OF ST PETER IN CHAINS: STATUE OF MOSES (Michelangelo)

97) CHURCH OF ST PETER IN CHAINS: THE EXTERIOR

99) CHURCH OF ST PETER IN CHAINS: ST PETER'S CHAINS

S. PIETRO IN VINCOLI

The Church of S. Pietro in Vincoli is not far away from S. Maria; you take Via Cavour, after arriving to Largo Visconti di Venosta, you emerge on Piazza S. Pietro in Vincoli. On the left is the Church of **"S. Pietro in Vincoli"** (97) also called Basilica Eudoxiana, which was founded in 442 by Eudoxia, wife of the Emperor Valentinian III, as a shrine for the **"Chains of St Peter"** (99). The **Basilica Eudoxiana** was consecrated by Pope Sixtus II in 439 and was restored several times in the course of the centuries. The famous Chains of St Peter were found at Jerusalem and presented to Eudoxia by her mother Eudocia, wife of Theodosius II. At the base of the Mausoleum of Julius II — commissioned of Michelangelo by this Pope — stands out the **"Statue of Moses"** (98), the most important fragment of the Tomb, which was dismembered by Leo X. Some fragments are in Paris, others in Florence.

100) BASILICA OF ST JOHN LATERAN: THE MAJESTUOUS EXTERIOR ▶

THE BASILICA OF ST JOHN LATERAN

The „**Basilica of St. John Lateran**" (100) is the cathedral of Rome and the most ancient of the Patriarchal Basilicae. Commissioned by Pope Melchiades, it was begun in 311 and consecrated in 314. In order to arrive at Lateran, you have to take the straight line Via Merulana, which emerges exactly on the Piazza S. Giovanni in Laterano. Here

101) BASILICA OF ST JOHN LATERAN: THE CLOISTER

102) BASILICA OF ST JOHN LATERAN: INTERIOR

103) THE "SCALA SANTA" (HOLY STAIRCASE)

THE BASILICA OF ST PAUL OUTSIDE THE WALLS

In chronological order, it is the "third patriarchal basilica" in Rome, having been erected in 386 by the Emperor Valentinian II. On the same site Constantine had built a little basilica. The basilica of St Paul is the second-largest church in Rome — St Peter is the largest — and it is situated on the **Via Ostiense** (from which it derives the name of **Basilica Ostiense)** about one miles from Porta S. Paolo. What can be admired now has nothing of the original splendour. Entering by the four-arched Portico, you

104) BASILICA OF ST PAUL-OUTSIDE-THE-WALLS: THE CLOISTER

we shall see some of the Lateran Palaces (splendid museums) and the **Baptistery**, whereas the **"Main Façade"** (100) is on the side of Porta S. Giovanni. It was the **Holy See** before Gregory XI took it back — after the Avignon period — to Rome in the Vatican Palaces, and then transferred the "Chair" to St Peter. Lateran was an admirable residence — see the **"Chiostro"** (cloister) (101) — and a magnificent cathedral. The interior (102) consists of an austere and dignified nave with two aisles on either side, and with a cosmatesque pavement and a wooden ceiling, executed in 1500.

Five Councils were held in the Lateran Palaces between 1123 and 1517 (all ecumenical)and in 1929 the so-called "Lateran Treaty" which put an end to the dissension between the State and the Church, was signed here. In close proximity to the Lateran, you should also visit the **"Scala Santa"** (103) which, according to tradition, should be the staircase of the Pilatus Palace in Jerusalem, which Christ ascended the day of the sacrifice.

106) BASILICA OF ST PAUL-OUTSIDE-THE-WALLS: THE MOSAIC OF THE APSE

find yourselves before the **"Façade"** of the Basilica with its "Mosaics" (105) representing the blessing Christ between St Peter and St Paul. In the foreground, still in the photo (105), is the statue of St Paul by Giuseppe Obici. The splendid **"interior"** with a nave and two aisles on either side (107) re-echoes vaguely the original splendour, which still survives intact in the "Mosaics of the Apse" (106) where the figure of the blessing Jesus stands out. The mosaics go back to about 1200. You should also visit the "Cloister" (104) by Vassalletto which dates from 1214.

As its name is telling us, this basilica is dedicated to **St Paul**, suddenly converted to Christianity on the way to Damascus, where he was going in order to try the followers of Jesus Christ, after Christ had appeared to him asking: "Saul, why persecutest thou me...". It was the year A.D. 36. Saul became a Christian, changed his name to that of **Paul** and became the **Apostle of the Gentiles** (so the pagans were called). He suffered martyrdom in Rome, under Nero, in A.D. 67.

105) BASILICA OF ST PAUL-OUTSIDE-THE-WALLS: INTERIOR OF THE FOUR-ARCHED PORTICO WITH A STATUE OF ST PAUL AND MOSAIC DECORATIONS OF THE FAÇADE (p. opposite)

ROME IN CIVILISATION

Rome has a particular place in the history of civilization conceived as town, and hence as social, development. Indeed, just because it has been the capital of the ancient world and because it has become the capital of the contemporary world, Rome has never been able to profit from examples of others, except perhaps from extemporary and transient ones. Everything, which has been done in Rome, has been the fruit of spontaneous growth, and the external contributions, which have naturally not failed, have been amalgamated not only with the local reality, but also with its spirit of coherent contradiction.

The contradiction is only apparent. It is right, we think, to speak of coherent contradiction, since Rome stands before us to suggest various examples of it. Its splendours, its declines, its continuous revivals as a great cosmopolitan city, all these are examples of coherent contradiction. It had a million inhabitants in the IInd century of the Empire, but three centuries later its population had dwindled to less than 30.000. With the accession of the papacy to the government of the city, Rome experienced a new revival, but the barbarian invasions devastated it to such an extent that, as history says, it was left completely deserted. Rome, however, recovered, and when, in the 9th century, the Emperor Charlemagne dignified it, by bringing back the rites of coronation, it awoke to new splendours.

It suffered another invasion in 1084 and was again depopulated under oppressive Norman rule, but later it recovered with the rise of the Communes. However, with the voluntary exile to Avignon of Pope Clement X, which was continued by John XXII, Benedict XII and Gregory XI — who brought back the Holy See to Rome — the city was, between 1305 and 1377, once more emptied; to such an extent that, as we have already seen, goats were pasturing on the Capitol and on St Peter's Square.

After overcoming the dramatic phase of the "Sack of Rome" in 1527 by the Lansquenets,

Rome returned, under the impulse of the Renaissance, to the splendours of the past. And from that period on, the ascending march of the "Eternal City" has been more or less constant. But even out of its splendour itself, contradictions emerged. The Roman nobility took for its own the ancient monuments and, not always respecting their primitive harmony, transformed them into dwelling-houses. In this way, the Arch of Janus became a fortress, deprived of all the statues in the niches; the Teatre of Marcellus, a dwelling-house; to erect the new Basilica of St Peter, Bramante pulled down the pre-existing one which dated from 324, thus deserving rightly the name of "Ruining Master"; the Barberini and Pope Urban VIII destroyed very ancient Roman vestiges, plundering them to get construction stones for their palaces and for St Peter. Last but not least, the vicissitudes of the Colosseum which became a travertine quarry.

Contradictions, we said: because Bramante was a great architect; the Orsini family, very munificent; the Barberini, great aristocrats and popes. Amidst such blows, Rome continued undaunted on the way of civilization: its own civilization which is unique in the world. There is a period in the history of Rome which is trully characterized by an impressive eagerness for the works and creations of the greatest artists. Princes of the Church and Popes called to Rome Giotto, Raphael, Michelangelo, Bramante, Alexander Galilei (built the façade of St John Lateran), Giacomo della Porta and Domenico Fontana, Pirro Ligorio, Carlo Maderno (who erected the façade of St Peter), Bernini, Canova, Nicolò Salvi, Taddeo Landini (Fontana delle Tartarughe), Francesco de Sanctis and hundreds of others who we cannot mention here for reason of synthesis. During the Renaissance period the city completed the layout of its monuments, assuming more and more a definite physiognomy. New roads, churches, palaces, were built, squares were opened on narrow sites.

What had been plundered and impoverished was put in order. All the monuments of Republican and Imperial Rome were restored. Apart from the "Fora" and the other antiquities of Rome such as the "Piramide Cestia", the "Mausoleum of Augustus", the "Baths of Diocletian" and so on, the Rome of your dream, the Rome long cherished by poets, writers, musicians, painters and other talents, the romantic Rome of tourists, pilgrims and young honeymooning couples, was born in that period. It is Renaissance Rome, Rome created by the bounteousness of religious and secular princes, this Rome destined to become once again a great metropolis.

The spendid staircase that leads up to the church of S. Maria d'Aracoeli was built in the middle of the 14th century; the Sistine Chapel is of the middle of the 15th century; the Capitoline Palaces with the gorgeous square of Michelangelo belong to the 16th century. St Peter's Square by Gian Lorenzo Bernini goes back to the 17th century. The same Bernini is the author of the ten dazzling statues of angels which adorn the bridge of Castel Sant'Angelo. Still to the 17th century belong the very famous **Piazza Navona** and the churches of "S. Ivo alla Sapienza", "S. Andrea delle Fratte", and "S. Carlino alle 4 Fontane" by Francesco Borromini. The 18th century is characterized by the construction of the sublime "Scalinata di Trinità dei Monti"; the spectacular "Fontana di Trevi", the "Palazzo Doria Panphili". "Piazza di Spagna", too, has been laid out during this period, whereas the "Fontana della Barcaccia" by Pietro Bernini, father of the great Gian Lorenzo, had already been installed in 1627-29. Giuseppe Valadier laid out in 1800 "Piazza del Popolo" in an insuperable manner, and tied his name to the Pincio where he erected the "Casina Valadier". The headquarters of the Bank of Italy, the majestic "Via Veneto", the "Piazza dell'Esedra" (today Piazza della Repubblica), the beautiful "Fontana delle Najadi" (erected after various interruptions between 1855 and 1914) and the "Palazzo di Giustizia" popularly called the "Palazzaccio", were all built between the end of the 19th century and the beginning of the 20th. The culture of an epoch or of a cosmopolitan city like Rome is not marked only by the works of art, the villas, the squares, the monuments etc. A culture is made by men and by the surroundings they lived in: like Via Margutta which has become an open-air art gallery; like "Via Condotti" with the famous "Caffè Greco" that housed Goethe, Gogol, Schopenauer, Stendhal, Ippolito Taine, Baudelaire, Berlioz, Mendelssohn, Bartholdy, Wagner, the divine Liszt, the terrible Anatole France and Leopardi, Di Giacomo, Pascarella, D'Annunzio etc.; like Piazza Navona with the sale of toys at the end of the year and at the Epiphany; like Trastevere with the popular and very nice "Festa de noantri". And "Porta Portese" 'and its little market, and "Piazza Campo dei Fiori", and finally, the music of Rome, the "Ponentino", and last but not least, the mild climate with the enchanting sunsets on the Tiber.

The "History of a Civilization" is the history of man who lives his everyday life, in all its manifestations. It is the history of what man does and of what man thinks. In ultimate analysis, it is his contribution to the sociality in which he finds himself. Rome is social like few other towns in the world: it is perhaps the strongest centre of attraction one can think of, because the motives of such attraction are multifarious and because Rome can satisfy the most different needs. "To live in Rome" is not like living in other towns: you come to it attracted by various inducements — spiritual, cultural, historical, artistic — and you stop in it overwhelmed by a charm which radiates from every monument, from every church, from all the roads and from the people.

Having left the Termini Station, let us set about to visit this marvellous city, entering by that natural vestibule, the **Piazza dell'Esedra** (or **della Repubblica**) (108) opened by Gaetano Koch in 1870. In the middle is the

108) PIAZZA DELL'ESEDRA OR DELLA REPUBBLICA

109) FOUNTAIN OF THE NAIADES: DETAIL

famous **"Fountain of the Naiads"** of which, in the photo (109), we van see one of the four bronze groups that surround it, a work by Mario Rutelli who also designed the central group. A few yards walk and we arrive at the **"Fontana dell'Aqua Felice"** (110), so called because Pope Sixtus (Felice Peretti) commissioned it of Domenico Fontana in 1585. The church of **"S. Maria delle Vittorie"** is a work by Maderno who erected it between 1608 and 1620. A few steps along Via XX Settembre and **Via Quirinale** (111) and you can see the residence of the Head of the Italian Republic as well as the beautiful **Fountain of the Dioscuri,** the statues of which date from the Imperial age. We then return to Largo S. Susanna and ascend Via Barberini, till we arrive in Piazza Barberini, from which will begin what we have chosen to call a **"Romantic Itinerary".** With such an itinerary we are intending to offer visitors a Roman excursion without bothering them with too

80

110) FOUNTAIN OF THE "HAPPY WATER" AND CHURCH OF S. MARIA DELLA VITTORIA

111) PIAZZA DEL QUIRINALE AND PALACE OF THE HEAD OF STATE

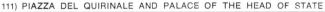

many technico-historical dates, references and names, which may turn a visit to Rome into an encyclopedical bath, perhaps interesting from an intellectual point of view, but with very low emotional content.

The itinerary we are suggesting to you is of a sentimental nature: a journey through Renaissance Rome which will concentrate on what one should see rather than on what one should know, which will make the heart work rather than the mind and which will remain in your heart even when the memory of it shall have become in time only a sensation.

The Rome which a song, two notes on the piano, the tune of a mandolin can bring to mind: the Rome which is called Villa Borghese, Trinità dei Monti, Piazza di Spagna, Piazza Navona, Fontana di Trevi, Trastevere... In short a

THE ROMANTIC ITINERARY

to see that Rome "of your dream" which will always remain in your heart.

81

112) FOUNTAIN OF THE TRITONE IN THE BARBERINI SQUARE (Bernini) ▶

114) VIA VENETO WITH PORTA PINCIANA

Having looked very attentively at the celebrated **"Fontana del Tritone"** (112) by Bernini (1632-37), we now take the splendid "Via Veneto" (113) opened at the beginning of the century. It is a large arterial street, bordered with trees and flanqued by remarquable palaces, with many bars and first class hotels (in the foreground we are seeing **Palazzo Margherita** standing in a garden, now the seat of the American Embassy). At its beginning, there is the **Church of** the Capuchin Friars. The Via ends at **"Porta Pinciana"**, behind which stretches one of the most beautiful villas in Rome: Villa Borghese.

VILLA BORGHESE

Villa Borghese was created at the beginning of the 17th century by Pope Paul V who put it at the disposal of his nephew, Cardinal Caffarelli. It underwent various

113) VIA VENETO: AT NIGHT

alterations and enlargements till it became the largest park in Rome. Since 1902 it has been 'a public park. At Villa Borghese we will find a large riding ground "Piazza di Siena" where various horse-races are held, the celebrated "Galleria Borghese" containing various art treasures, as well as the National Gallery of Modern Art. After passing Porta Pinciana and Piazzale Brasile, we take Via San Paolo del Brasile which opens before us and, a few yards farther on, we turn right into "Viale del Museo Borghese". At the end of the avenue we will find **"Galleria Borghese"** (115) which was the richest private collection in the world. It was bought by the State in 1902. Both the **Museum** and the **Galleria Borghese** are housed in the same place; the Museum is on the first floor and the Gallery, on the second. Within the Museum, in the first room on the right after the portico, we will find the **"Sala della Paolina"** (117) and, following immediately after, the **"Sala del David"** (116). The statue, of rare elegance and beauty, which represents Paolina Bonaparte, sister of Napoleon, was sculptured in 1805 by Antonio Canova who called it the "Victorious Venus". She was the wife of Camillo Borghese who married her in second marriage in 1803. The "David" is a work of the young Gian Lorenzo Bernini, sculptured between 1623 and 1624 on commission by the first owner of Villa Borghese, the Cardinal Scipione Caffarelli-Borghese. Of course, many other works of this Museum deserve our attention: "Apollo and Daphne", the "Rapt of Proserpina" (both by Bernini) and, in the Gallery, the "Descent from the Cross" (Raphael), "Diana the Huntress" (Domenichino), the "Madonna of the Serpent" (Caravaggio), the "Sacred Love and Profane Love" by Titian, the "Danae" of Correggio and still in the Museum of which we have seen only the "David" and the "Paolina" the "Dancing Faun", a copy from an original sculpture by Lysippus. Note also the very beautiful group "Apollo and Daphne", a work by Gian Lorenzo Bernini. The Museum, however, as well as the Gallery, deserves an attentive and diligent visit.

115) BORGHESE GALLERY: THE EXTERIOR

116) BORGHESE GALLERY: THE DAVID

117) The Borghese Gallery, Paolina Bonaparte

117 bis) The little lake of Villa Borghese.

THE PINCIO

After visiting the Gallery of Modern Art, you take the Viale di Valle Giulia which joins Viale Pietro Canonica and then, from the Viale delle Magnolie you arrive at the "Pincio", the very beautiful public park laid out by Valadier and finished between 1809 and 1814. On the left you find the famous "Casina Valadier", and on the right, in close proximity to the "lift" which from the **Pincio** takes you to the Viale del Muro Torto is the famous **"Orologio ad Acqua"** (Water clock) (118). You should also note the Monument to **Enrico Toti** and the **"Fontana del Mosè salvato dalle Acque"** (Fountain of Moses saved from the Waters). The Pincio ends with the terrace

118) "OROLOGIO AD ACQUA"
WATER CLOCK OF THE PINCIO ▶

119) THE PEOPLE SQUARE (PIAZZA DEL POPOLO)

of "Piazzale Napoleone" from which you can enjoy a **splendid view** of Rome and of Piazza del Popolo, especially beautiful at sunset.

The "Piazzale Napoleone" is the natural meeting place for the "lovers" of Rome, that is for those people who come to Rome attracted by its natural beauties half-hidden in magic architectonic surroundings which make them still more suggestive and make a sunset from the Pincio a uniquely beautiful experience.

You go quickly down Viale D'Annunzio and arrive on the **Piazza del Popolo** (119) of which we have already admired the view.

This square, like the Pincio, is due to the art of Giuseppe Valadier who laid it out between 1816 and 1820. Its form is oval and it is limited to the east and the west by two "Exedras". The **Obelisk of Flaminius** is placed in the middle of the square; the obelisk is said to be one of the most ancient monuments in Rome. To the south, at the beginnings of **Viale del Corso** and **Viale del Babuino** are the celebrated churches of **S. Maria di Montesanto** and **S. Maria dei Miracoli.** In front of the latter, on the north side of the square, is the lovely church of **S. Maria del Popolo.**

88

PIAZZA DI SPAGNA

Our romantic itinerary is about to reach one of its central and most suggestive points: Piazza di Spagna. You go along Via del Babuino and you come across Piazza di Spagna of which we are showing you (120) a view at night together with the **"Fontana della Barcaccia"** by Pietro Bernini (sculptured between 1627 and 1629). The Piazza di Spagna is one of the places so dear to visitors of Rome; the dear and romantic centre of Papal and pre-risorgimento Rome. On the north side, the square is surrounded by 18th century palaces and adorned with palm-trees. It ends with the "Fontana della Barcaccia" and goes beyond it to the south, towards the Palazzo della Propaganda Fide. From the Fontana della Barcaccia, a marvellous and pictorial **"Scalinata"** (121) almost hangs, so to speak, the Piazza on the slopes of the Pincio. It culminates with the church of **"S. Trinità dei Monti"** (122) which was erected by Louis XII, King of France, and consecrated by Sixtus V in 1585. A centre of particular attraction, the Scalinata (which in the spring presents the lovely "infiorata") was built by Francesco De Sanctis in 1726.

From Piazza di Spagna, it is worth while going to Via Margutta (123), which during some month of the year is an authentic open-air art exhibition by artists who have

120) PIAZZA DI SPAGNA WITH FOUNTAIN OF THE BARCACCIA

122) THE CHURCH OF TRINITA' DEI MONTI

123) VIA MARGUTTA: BY NIGHT

their atelier in the neighbourhood. Another interesting and
necessary visit, since it lies on
our way, is **Via Condotti**, Via
della Fontanella Borghese, Via
del Clementino, then turn left
into Via della Scrofa and then
right into Via S. Agostino to
arrive, after a twenty minutes
walk from Piazza di Spagna,
across Renaissance and Baroque Rome, on Piazza Navona.

◀ 121) THE SCALINATA OF TRINITA' DEI MONTI

THE "INFIORATA"

PIAZZA NAVONA

Here we are, at the second key-point of our itinerary: **Piazza Navona** (124) is one of the places which are bound to remain impressed in the heart and mind of every visitor. The harmony of the lines, the harmonious lay-out of the palaces and the churches, the placing of three fountains at the centre, make it one of the most beautiful squares in Rome. Built on the site of the ancient Stadium of Diocletian, 240 m. long and 65 m. wide, it has in the middle the **"Fontana dei 4 Fiumi"** (125) which Bernini sculptured in 1651; on the north is the **"Fontana del Moro"** (126) designed by the same Bernini but modelled by Mari in 1655;

finally, on the south side, is the celebrated **"Fontana del Nettuno"** (127) designed and realized by Giacomo della Porta in 1574 and subsequently adorned with the statues of Antonio della Bitta in 1873. On the right side of the square, we have entered from the north, is the church of **"S. Agnese in Agone"** (127) brought to conclusion by Borromini in 1657.
Piazza Navona awakes the same emotions which have rendered famous the Piazza di Spagna. Situated at the heart of Renaissance Rome, surrounded by Palazzo Panphili, Palazzo Braschi, Palazzo Massimo, Palazzo Capranica, Palazzo della Sapienza etc. it is at the same time a square where popular celebrations are held, like the fair and the toy-market and the popular feast of the Epiphany.
Wearing in our heart the memory of the

125) PIAZZA NAVONA: THE FOUNTAIN OF THE FOUR RIVERS (detail)

126) PIAZZA NAVONA: THE FOUNTAIN OF THE MORO (detail)

128) PIAZZA COLONNA

Piazza Navona, we reach the **Palazzo Madama** (the seat of the Senate of the Republic) across the Corsia Agonale: by Via del Salvatore and Via Giustiniani we emerge on the **"Piazza Rotonda"** exactly in front of the **Pantheon** (page 19 and 20). From here several little roads lead us to the **Palazzo Montecitorio**, the seat of the Parliament. After passing, on the right of the Piazza Montecitorio, the Palazzo Wedekind, we arrive on the well known **"Piazza Colonna"** (128) which is one of the most frequented and lively places in Rome. The Piazza opens on the Via del Corso and in its centre towers the great **"Column of Marcus Aurelius"**, surmounted by the statue of St Paul. The column goes back to the 2nd century of the Empire, and was erected to commemorate the victories of Marcus Aurelius over the Germanic peoples.

95

129) FOUNTAIN OF TREVI: DETAIL

THE FOUNTAIN OF TREVI

Across the Corso and after taking first the Via de Sabili and then the following Via dei Crociferi, we reach the **Piazza di Trevi**, with the most famous **"Fontana di Trevi"** (129), (130) known in the whole world and visited each year by millions of tourists. It is the largest square in Rome and was built and designed by Nicolò Salvi on an order by Clement XII between 1732 and 1762. Salvi died in 1751 and Clement XIII brought the work to conclusion. The fountain was really born in 1453 when Nicholas V had the **conduits** of the aqueduct of the "Acqua Vergine" repaired, which Agrippina had built in 19 B.C. for his baths near the Pantheon. The original tank was by Leon Battista Alberti and the conduits of the aqueduct used to pass by **Via Condotti**, hence the name Condotti. Leaning against the Palace of the Dukes of Poli, the fountain is 20 m. wide and 26 high. At the centre, in the niche is the **statue of the Ocean** standing on the seashell pulled by sea-horses. In the two lateral niches are the statues of **"Abbondanza"** (left) and **"Salubrità"** (right). The coat of arms of the Orsini stands out on the cornice. According to tradition, he who throws a coin into the fountain is bound to come back to Rome. The little "Piazza di Trevi" which houses the fountain, is always crowded with people all year through. The tourist who, following the tradition, throws a coin into the fountain, is always followed by a little boy who fishes it up with the help of a magnet. But this, too, is part of the atmosphere which the tourist accepts willingly from this unpredictable Rome.

130) FOUNTAIN OF TREVI ▶

PIAZZA VENEZIA

From Piazza di Trevi to Piazza Venezia is quite a short way. You return to the Corso and walk along it, on the left side, till you arrive on the **"Piazza Venezia"** (131). It is another of those dynamic centres of the town, not only because of the history which surrounds it and the vicinity of the "Fora", but also because, being so near the Capitol, it is the administrative centre of Rome. All the larger roads of Rome converge to it: Via del Corso, Via IV Novembre, Via dei Fori Imperiali, Via Plebiscito and Via del Teatro di Marcello, which link the whole town with this area. The Piazza is limited on the sides by the **Palazzo delle Assicurazioni Generali**, facing which is the **"Palazzo Venezia"** (132), one of the first palaces of Renaissance Rome and today the seat of a Museum. It is attributed to Leon Battista Alberti, and has also been the residence of the Popes until 1564.

131) PIAZZA VENEZIA: GENERAL VIEW OF THE VITTORIANO

132) PIAZZA VENEZIA: PALAZZO VENEZIA

133) THE MONUMENT TO VITTORIO EMANUELE II

THE VITTORIANO

The Piazza Venezia is closed to the south by the candid and imposing mass of the "Monument to Vittorio Emanuele II" (134) also called "The Vittoriano", erected between 1885 and 1911 by the architect Sacconi to commemorate the unity of Italy. Built of white marble, instead of the usual travertine of all the ancient monuments in Rome, it creates a striking contrast with the ancient world that surrounds it (and which it dominates) in spite of its neo-classic lines.

In the centre of the staircase, there is the large statue of Rome, and at the foot of it, the grave of the Unknown Soldier. Above, towers the equestrian statue of Vittorio Emanuele II (133), where you arrive by ascending a few flights of stairs which converge towards the base of the statue, a work by Enrico Chiaradia. Other flights of stairs lead to the last external terrace from where you can enjoy a beautiful view of Piazza Venezia and Via del Corso. Then

from the lateral propylaea you can go to the semi-circular portico. From there you can enjoy a beautiful view of Rome, in particular of Via del Teatro Marcello, Aracoeli, Capitol from the propylaea on the right. From the propylaea on the left you can have a view of the "Via dei Fori Imperiali" (135), the Colosseum, the Forum of Trajan, the Forum of Augustus, and of Caesar as well as of the Oppio Hill. The "Istituto per la Storia del Risorgimento Italiano" as well as the "Museo Centrale del Risorgimento" has its seat in the Monument. The birth of the gigantic monument, which the then reigning dynasty had presented to Italy to commemorate the establishment of national unity, has been a source of many controversies which only time has put an end to. It deserves, however, an internal as well as external visit. Of particular interest ist the "Archivio" of the Museo Centrale del Risorgimento rich in more than 350.00 autographes and documents of the Risorgimento, and containing also the archives of Massimo d'Azeglio, Francesco Crispi, and Ricciotti Garibaldi, son of Giuseppe Garibaldi, the maker of the unity of Italy.

134) THE VITTORIANO

136) THE LUPA (WOLF)

THE CAPITOL

Our romantic itinerary is spangled with key-points: the Capitol is one of them, too. You arrive to it simply by descending from the Vittoriano and by turning left towards **Piazza dell'Aracoeli**. The Capitol — or the Capitoline Hill — is one of the "famous Seven Hills" of Rome and the one which has always housed the municipal administration . It is made up of two summits, on one of which the **"Chiesa dell'Aracoeli"** has been built (138) and on the other one are the "Palaces of the Capitol" (137). The two summits are separated by a depression, now occupied by the **"Piazza del Campidoglio"** (137). In ancient times, on the hill now occupied by the Capitoline Palaces stood the Temple of Jupiter, whereas on the summit now covered by the Church of the Aracoeli stood the Temple of Juno and Virtue. Only few evidences remain of these temples.

The Capitol is accessible by the staircase which leads to the Church of Aracoeli as well as by the beautiful Michelangelo's "Cordonata", which, in the form of a ramp, culminates in front of the monument of **"Marcus Aurelius"**. The Aracoeli was erected in ancient times and in 1250 it was almost completely rebuil by the Benedictines. The splendid staircase was built in 1348 and the first man to mount its steps was Cola di Rienzo, a Roman demagogue who the year before had become master of Rome.
From here you go down to the complex of the Capitoline Palaces: on the left we have the new Palace (or Museo Capitolino), in the background, the Palazzo Senatorio and on the right, the Palazzo dei Conservatori (which can be seen on page 105). The Palazzo Capitolino and the Palazzo dei Conservatori have been built, on designs by Michelangelo, respectively by Rainaldi (1655) and by Della Porta (1568), whereás the Palazzo Senatorio is due to a combined work of Rainaldi and Della Porta.
The **Piazza del Campidoglio** (Capitol's Square) (137) is one of the finest and fairest squares in Rome and is due to the insuper-

able art of Michelangelo Buonarroti who designed it, keeping in mind the necessity of harmony with the surrounding palaces. In the middle of the square stands the statue of **"Marcus Aurelius"** (142) installed here by Michelangelo in 1538. The lovely Michelangelo staircase looks conspicuous on the façade of the Palazzo Senatorio; it is flanqued by two statues: on the right, the

137) THE CAPITOLINE SQUARE   138) THE CHURCH OF ARACOELI AND THE CAPITOLIN (in the two following pages) ▶

statue of the **"Tiber"** (141); on the left, the statue of the **"Nile"** (139). At the centre, in a niche beneath the staircase, there is the statue of **"Minerva"** (140). These statues come from the baths of Constantine on the Quirinal.

We have to specify that the river "Tiber" was once the river "Tigre". You can also note that the statue of **Marcus Aurelius** comes from the lawn in front of St John Lateran. It was saved from the destructive fury against Pagan things following the edict of 394 against Pagan rites, owing to the fact that it was taken to be a statue of Constantine.

139) THE STATUE OF THE "NILO"

140) THE STATUE OF MINERVA   141) THE STATUE OF THE TIBER   142) THE EQUESTRIAN STATUE OF MARCUS AURELIUS ▶

THE CAPITOLINE MUSEUMS

The **"Musei Capitolini"** are the oldest collection of works of art in the world. The collection was begun by Pope Sixtus IV in 1471 and was subsequently continued by other popes. It develops in the three sections of the Palazzo Nuovo (the true Capitoline Museum) and of the Palazzo dei Conservatori which house the „Sale dei Conservatori" and the "Pinacoteca Capitolina". Within the **Capitoline Museum** we will see the **"Bust of Brutus"** (143) in the room of the gladiator. In the "Sale dei Conservatori" there is the famous little statue of the **"Spinario"** (144). Other rooms also deserve a visit: there is the "Sala dei Trionfi di Mario" and then in the homonymous room you will see **"La lupa Capitolina"** (the Capitoline Wolf) (136); in the "Pinacoteca" we shall see, among other paintings, **"The Sybil"** (145) by Domenichino and the **"G. Giovannino"** (146) by Caravaggio, both in the "VIIth Sala di S. Petronilla".

A visit to the Capitoline Museums should, naturally, be accurate and detailed, but this book is not a guide and, therefore, we must go on to know other aspects of Rome.

From the Capitol, by Via del Teatro di Marcello (seen at page 17) you arrive on the "Piazza Bocca della Verità" where, together with the ancient Temples of the "Fortuna Virilis" (page 18) and "Vesta" (at page 18).

143) THE CAPITOLINE MUSEUM: BUST OF BRUTUS

144) THE CAPITOLINE MUSEUM: THE "SPINARIO" (Sala dei Conservatori)

145) THE CAPITOLINE MUSEUM: THE SYBIL (Domenichino) (Pinacoteca)

146) THE CAPITOLINE MUSEUM: S. GIOVANNINO (Caravaggio) (Pinacoteca)

146bis) THE CAPITOLINE MUSEUM: THE MOSAICS

148) THE BOCCA DELLA VERITA'

rises the majestuous and sublime church of **"S. Maria in Cosmedin"** (147).

Here you should not neglect seeing, and putting your hand into, the **"Bocca della Verità"** (148) and (149), which is in the portico facing the church. The Church belongs to the 6th century and was various times enlarged until the actual façade was erected in the 18th century; the Romanesque bell-tower dates from the 12th century.

149) THE ATRIUM OF THE "BOCCA DELLA VERITA'"

TRASTEVERE

The "Ponte Cestio" takes you to the "Isola in Trastevere", the most famous, the most Roman and the most lively district of Rome, where, each year, the "Festa de noantri" with dancing, music, fireworks and banquets is held. The feast takes place in the Viale Trastevere (which can be reached by walking along the Lungotevere dell'Anguillara) in July and lasts a month.

In Trastevere, you should not neglect visiting the Church of **"S. Maria di Trastevere"** (151) and the Church of P. Pietro in Montorio in the vicinity of which there is the **"Fontanone dell'Acqua Paola"** (152). From the enchanting Janiculum Promenade, you reach the **"Monument to Garibaldi"** (153) from the terrace of which you can enjoy a magnificent view of Rome. A visit to **"Porta Portese"** and to its **"Mercatino"** (154) closes the walk.

From Piazza Bocca della Verità you walk along the Lungo Tevere dei Pierleoni till you arrive at the beginning of the "Ponte Fabricio", in front of the Teatro di Marcello, after passing the Church of S. Nicola in Carcere. The bridge, the oldest in Rome, having been built by the Consul Fabricius in 62 B.C., leads to the **"Isola Tiberina"** (150), on which stands the Church of S. Bartolomeo, going back to the 10th century.

150) THE BROKEN BRIDGE AND THE TIBER ISLAND   151) THE CHURCH OF S. MARIA IN COSMEDIN ▶

152) THE FONTANONE DELL'ACQUA PAOLA

153) MONUMENT TO GARIBALDI ON THE JANICULUM

154) THE LITTLE MARKET OF PORTA PORTESE

Our "romantic itinerary" has come to an end. Let us go back over the Tiber (over the Garibaldi Bridge) and then to the **"Synagogue"** (156) across the Lungotevere dei Cenci. From here, let us proceed into the many-coloured, phantasmagoric "Jewish District" which ends with the Piazza Mattei where after passing by the historical "Portico of Octavia" you will see the most lovely **"Fontana delle Tartarughe"** (Fountain of the Tortoises) (155). The Fountain is by Taddeo who erected it in 1581. On going back to Termini, let us give a look at Lyric Rome with its natural temple, the **,,Teatro dell'Opera"** (157), built in 1880 on Via del Viminale. From here to the Termini Station, from where our excursion started, the way is very short.

156) THE SYNAGOGUE

157) THE THEATRE OF THE OPERA

159) THE "FONTANA DELL'ORGANO" WITH VIEW OF THE PARK

THE VILLA D'ESTE

Lying around Rome are beautiful and numerous "Patrician Villas" which may attract the attention of tourists.

We will briefly concentrate our attention on **"Villa d'Este"** at Tivoli, famous in the whole world for its splendid fountains. The Villa, formerly a convent, was sumptuously rebuilt about 1550 and continuously embellished, till it came to be considered one of the most beautiful and aristocratic residences in the world, above all for its splendid gardens in which more than **500 fountains** stand. The finest of these fountains is certainly the one called **"Dell'Organo"** (158) and (159), which is accessible by the lovely **"Viale delle Cento Fontane"** (160).

160) THE AVENUE OF "100 FONTANE"

CONTEMPORARY ROME

We have seen ancient Rome; we have walked together through modern Rome born of the splendours of the Renaissance, but there still remains another aspect of Rome which cannot be neglected: It is contemporary Rome born under the impulse of economic recovery, which followed the tragic second world war. Spurred by manias for grandeur and using certain dubious ways, this Rome has tried to imitate Imperial Rome and to recapture the greatness of a still near historical past, but without succeeding in the least. History has its necessity and does not know any return.

It is, nevertheless, a Rome which ought to be known, if only for that comparison which is the source of stimulating intuitions. And so, to the Rome of the monumental vestiges, to Renaissance and Baroque Rome, which has made much of the history of this city, let us add also this Rome of the straight lines, in which, however, the longing for the arch is still alive. The EUR is a valid testimony of that; especially in some constructions — see in the detail the **"Palazzo della Civiltà del Lavoro"** (Palace of the Civilization of Work" (162) — with which a modern interpretation of the historical Colosseum has been attempted.

Of course, the EUR has not all been built in the same manner. It was begun as the permanent seat of the "Olimpiade della Civiltà" in 1938. First the war and then the new administration immediately after the war, forced the abandonment of the original plan, which did not exclude the possibility of an urban expansion of Rome towards the sea.

161 bis) A NIGHT VIEW OF THE EUR

It was, especially, this second aspect of the plan to determine, seven years after the war, the resumption of the works to build a residential and administrative centre of great importance. The palaces of "littorio" type were completed and destined to public uses. Of the "Palazzo della Civitlà del Lavoro" we have already written. Situated in front of the opposite heading of the junction street, the other palace has been destined to receptions and congresses.

162) EUR: THE PALAZZO DELLA CIVILTA' DEL LAVORO

163) EUR: THE LITTLE LAKE BEFORE THE PALACE OF THE ENI IN THE BACKGROUND ON THE LEFT THE CHURCH OF ST PETER AND ST PAUL

165) THE LEONARDO DA VINCI AIRPORT: THE HALL WITH A VIEW OF THE CONTROL TOWER

166) THE FARNESINA PALACE: THE FOREIGN OFFICE

Today, various government departments have their seat at the EUR, in modern and well built palaces; and, then, there is the Alitalia, the ENI, a splendid **"Palazzo dello Sport"** (Sport Palace) (161), a characteristic restaurant **"a fungo"** (Mushroom) (161). In the middle lies a tranquil and blue artificial lake. You should also visit the Church of St Peter and St. Paul.

Other Roman "modern constructions" are the underground, which takes you from Termini to the EUR, and the building complex of the "Foro Italico" in the Monte Mario area, where numerous sport installations are to be found, among which the best known is certainly the **"Stadio dei Marmi"** (167) designed by Del Debbio. In front of the "Stadio" is the **"Stadio del 100.000"** (168). By going on along the Lungotevere Diaz, after coming out of the Forum, you will meet the Palazzo della Farnesina, the seat of the **"Foreign Office"** (166). The large and very modern "Fiumicino Airport" dedicated to Leonardo Da Vinci, is situated practically on the sea, 28 km from Rome, in the Ostia

164) THE LEONARDO DA VINCI AIRPORT: THE STATUE OF LEONARDO

167) THE ITALIAN FORUM. THE "STADIO DEI MARMI"

168) THE ITALIAN FORUM: THE "STADIO DEI 100.000"

169) THE TERMINI STATION

area and has two runways, 4 and 2,6 km long. The airport complex is composed of the "Airstation", the 'Control Tower", 45 m high, and a splendid waiting-hall, provided with all comforts. In the photo, we are seeing the "Statue of Leonardo" (164) and the "Hall" (165) with a view of the "Control Tower".

THE TERMINI STATION

Here we are back at the Termini Station. This magnificent station, the hall of which is 419 feet long, was begun before the second world war, but was completed only in 1950. We have left the renowned **"Termini Station"** (169) at the end, because, if it is true that visits to towns begin after the arrival at the station, it is none the less true that it is from the station that one takes leave of the town just visited. Our last photograph has this sense of "Arrivederci Roma" ("Good-bye Rome").

In compiling this book, we have been thinking of the tourist who wants to take with him, from Rome, not only a series of beautiful photographs or a more or less handy guide-book, but also a joyous, lively, warm remembrance of this marvellous city unequalled in the world.

At home, when reading through the pages of this book, the walks you have taken, the things you have seen, the monuments you have visited, will come back to you, but they will come back in an ordered, logical manner, destined, therefore, to remain for ever in your mind and in your heart. The "dream" of the Eternal City will come alive under your eyes and those of the persons dear to you, who will enjoy with you the charm of this unforgettable city.

127

TABLE OF CONTENTS

How to use this Book . . . . . . Page 2
ROME IN HISTORY
The legend of the foundation of Rome » 3
The legend of the seven kings . . . » 3
The history of Republican Rome . . » 3
The conquest of the Mediterranean countries . . . . » 4
The birth of the Roman Empire . . . » 4
The fall of the Roman Empire . . . » 5
Monuments of ancient Rome . . . . » 6
The Arch of Septimius Severus and Temple of Saturn . . . . » 7
The Temple of Castor and Pollux and Temple of the Vestals . . . . . » 8
The house of the Vestals and the Temple of Antoninus and Faustina . . . . » 9
The Arch of Titus and the Sacred Way . » 10
The **Palatine**, the Circus Maximus and the Trajan Markets . . . . . » 11
The Column of Trajan and the Basilica Ulpia . . . . » 12
The Basilica of Maxentius . . . . » 13
The **Colosseum** . . . . » 14
The Colosseum, exterior and interior . » 15
The **Arch of Constantine** . . . . » 16
The Theatre of Marcellus, the Temple of Apollo Sosianus and the Temple of Vesta . . . . » 17
The Temple of Fortuna Virilis and the Baths of Caracalla . . . . . . » 18
The **Pantheon**, interior . . . . . » 19
The Pantheon, exterior and the "Pulcin of Minerva" . . . . » 20
The Tomb of Cecilia Metella and the Ancient Appian Way . . . . . » 21
The Pyramide of Caius Cestius and St Paul's Door (Porta S. Paolo) . . . . » 22
ROME RECONSTRUCTED . . . . » 22
A reconstruction of the Roman Forum » 23
A view of ROME RECONSTRUCTED . » 24-25
Fight of Gladiators and Martyrdom of Christians in the Colosseum . . . . » 26
Reconstruction of the Colosseum and the Arch of Constantine . . . . . » 27
The Basilica of Maxentius and the House of the Vestals . . . . » 28
The Forum of Augustus and the Forum of Trajan . . . . » 29
The Baths of Trajan and the Temple of Venus and Rome with the Colosseum » 30
Chariot-races at the Colosseum and Roman Forum . . . . » 31
ROME IN CHRISTIANITY . . . . » 32
Castel Sant'Angelo . . . . . . » 35

The **Basilica of St Peter** . . . . . » 37
St Peter's Square . . . . . . » 38
Paul VI at the window . . . . . » 40
Second Ecumenical Vatican Council . » 42
The **Pietà** of Michelangelo . . . . » 46
The Vatican City . . . . . . » 48
The Vatican Gardens . . . . . » 49
The **Sistine Chapel** . . . . . . » 53
The "Last Judgment" . . . . . . » 56
The "Volta" . . . . » 60
The Vatican Museum: the Pinacoteca (Picture Gallery) . . . . . . » 65
The Chapel of S. Nicolò . . . . » 66
The Museum Chiaramonti . . . . » 67
The **Basilica of S. Maria Maggiore** . . » 68
The Church of S. Prassede . . . » 70
The Basilica of St Peter in Chains . . » 70
The **Moses** . . . . » 71
The **Basilica of St John Lateran** . . . » 73
The **Basilica of St Paul-outside-the-Walls** » 75
ROME IN CIVILIZATION . . . . » 78
A "Romantic Itinerary" . . . . . » 81
The Triton Fountain and the Barberini Square . . . . » 82
Via Veneto . . . . » 83
Villa Borghese . . . . » 85
The Pincio . . . . » 86
The People's Square (Piazza del Popolo) » 88
Piazza di Spagna . . . . . . » 89
Trinità dei Monti . . . . . . » 90
Piazza Navona . . . . » 93
Piazza Colonna . . . . » 95
Fountain of Trevi . . . . . . » 96
Piazza Venezia . . . . » 98
The Vittoriano (the monument to Vittorio Emanuele II) . . . . . . » 99
Via dei Fori Imperiali . . . . . » 101
The **Capitol** . . . . » 102
The Capitol and the Church of Aracoeli 104-105
Marcus Aurelius . . . . . . » 107
The Capitoline Museums . . . . » 108
The Church of S. Maria in Cosmedin . » 110
The **"Bocca della Verità"** . . . . . » 111
Trastevere . . . . » 112
The Janiculum . . . . » 114
Porta Portese . . . . » 115
VILLA D'ESTE at Tivoli . . . . . » 119
A panoramic view on the EUR . . . 120-121
Contemporary Rome . . . . . » 122
The EUR . . . . » 123
The Leonardo Da Vinci Airport (Fiumicino) . . . . » 124
The Italian Forum . . . . . . » 125
The **Termini Station** . . . . . . » 127

L. 3.100 $ 5